MINIATURE P
WITH POLYMER CLAY

Sue Heaser

FARTHINGS PUBLISHING

The Farthings, Wortham Diss, Norfolk IP22 1PU

United Kingdom

Sue Heaser is a specialist in polymer clays and metal clays and has written 15 internationally published books on these and other craft subjects. She teaches workshops all over the world.

For information on Sue Heaser and her books visit:

www.sueheaser.com

CONTENTS

INTRODUCTION

Over the past 20 years I have written many dolls house and miniatures projects that have been published in a variety of magazines. This little book is a compilation of some of those projects that were first published in Dolls House and Miniature Scene magazine between about 2000 and 2010.

I have always enjoyed making more unusual miniatures with polymer clay. Many people use the clays to make miniature food but often they do not realise how amazing the material is for making a far wider range of miniatures. The clays simulate metal, wood, china and even fabric to perfection – often looking more realistic than the real material because of the scale. The miniatures in this collection are an exploration of "other things besides food" that you can make with polymer clay and I hope they will open your eyes to the exciting possibilities so you can go on to design and create your own miniature projects.

The best plan with this sort of polymer clay miniature is to make the components of the model separately, bake them, and then assemble them into the finished result. This moves away from the normal process of making the entire piece before baking. The technique gives wonderful opportunities for making professional-looking models that can even be given moving parts such as the Gramophone (with a winding handle), the Wood burner stove (with hinged doors) and the Library Globe which can be spun.

All the miniatures in this book are made in the standard dolls house scale of 1:12 or 1 inch to 1 foot. This means that they can be displayed in a dolls house but they also make delightful original gifts and ornaments. The projects are in a range of abilities from beginners to more advanced. The easier projects are arranged first so if you are a beginner, those are the ones to begin with.

HOW TO USE THIS BOOK

TEMPLATES AND PATTERNS

Many of the projects have templates and printed images that are used for making the miniature projects. Use a photocopier or scanner to copy the templates and images at exactly the same scale as they are printed in the book. Photocopiers should be set to print at "Actual size" or 100%.

Alternately you can visit my website where the templates and images for this book are available for download directly onto your computer.

Go to: www.sueheaser.com and follow the menu to Sue Heaser's Books, then Polymer Clay Books and click on the link to Miniature Templates. You will be able to open the pdf for each project that has templates or patterns and print them with your printer. Make sure that you select "Actual size" or untick the "Fit to page" option when printing so that the pdf prints at the correct scale.

MATERIALS LISTS

To avoid repetition, the lists do not include the basic toolkit of:

Ceramic tile, craft knife, slicer blade, rolling pin, needles, paintbrushes. See Tools and Equipment on page 76 for details.

BASIC INFORMATION

Descriptions of all the main Materials, Tools and Equipment are given at the end of the book along with basic techniques for working with polymer clay.

If you are a beginner, then read through these sections first.

The Kitchen Scales project, Page 61

DELFT TILES

Ceramic tiles add delightful details to a dolls house, whether in the bathroom, kitchen or around a fireplace. This project uses a wonderful product called Lazertran Silk, which allows you to transfer tile designs onto a sheet of polymer clay which is then cut up and baked to make little tiles in 1:12 scale. You can choose to make your tiles individually to arrange yourself when you glue them to the dolls house wall, or make them in a single panel.

The designs shown here are based on original Delft and polychrome tiles which have been popular from medieval times to the present day and would be suitable for any period of dolls house.

Expertise level: this is an easy project suitable for beginners.

TOOLS AND MATERIALS

- Polymer Clay - 56g (2oz) block of white
- Lazertran Silk paper – available from many art and craft suppliers or see www.lazertran.com
- Tile patterns photocopied onto Lazertran paper - See Step 1
- Rolling strips of thick cardboard about 2mm (1/12 in) thick for rolling an even sheet (or use a pasta machine set at this thickness).
- Gloss varnish - acrylic or water based
- PVA Glue
- Tile grout if required

THE PATTERNS

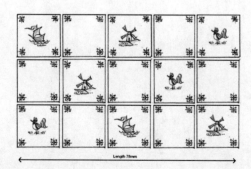

Length 78mm

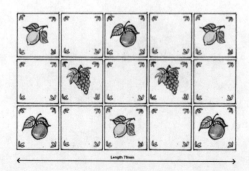

Length 78mm

6

Step 1

Use a colour photocopier to copy the tile patterns onto Lazertran Silk paper. Any high street copy shop will do this for you. Note that you need a laser printer with toner - not an ink jet printer for this to work.

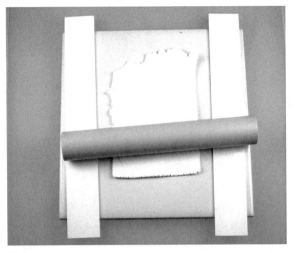

Step 2

Cut out the printed tile image on the Lazertran Silk paper leaving a small border all round.

Step 3

Knead about half the block of clay in your hands to warm and condition it before rolling into a sheet. It is easier to do this if you cut off small pieces and roll them into logs to soften the clay and then combine them into a single piece. Roll out the clay between the two strips of card so that your rolling pin rests on the card as you roll and the clay is an even thickness all across the sheet.

Step 4

Lay the sheet of clay on the tile and place the printed Lazertran paper on top, face down. Rub over the back with your finger to ensure it is firmly pressed onto the clay all over. You can roll over it with your rolling pin as well but do not squash the clay so much that it becomes misshapen.

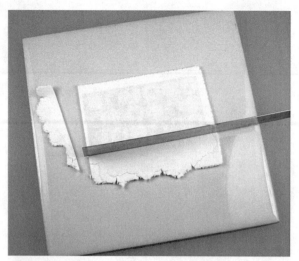

Step 5

Trim the clay sheet round the outside of the paper leaving a small border and set the tile aside for 30 minutes for the ink to penetrate the polymer clay.

Step 6

Now submerge the tile with the clay and paper on it in a sink or pan full of water. The water will not harm the polymer clay. Leave for 2 minutes and then swirl the water around. The paper will float off the clay leaving the image behind. Remove the tile from the water and mop away excess water carefully with a tissue or kitchen paper.

Step 7

Use the slicer blade to trim round the edge close to the image. Then cut along the lines between the tiles using the printed image as a guide. If you want to use the tiles as a complete panel, just mark between the lines with the blade and do not cut through. Leave the tiles on the ceramic tile without moving them - they can be separated after baking and if you move them now, they will distort.

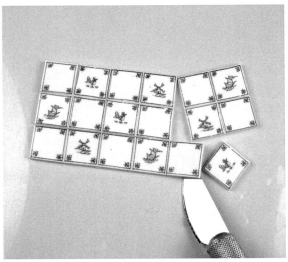

Step 8

Bake the clay on the ceramic tile (see Baking on page 75) and leave to cool. Varnish with gloss varnish and leave to dry. Slip a blade under the little tiles to free them as a whole panel, or snap them apart if you want to use them individually.

Now you can use PVA glue to attach them to your dolls house bathroom or kitchen wall. If you glue each tile individually, you can grout the finished tiled area just like full size tiles if you wish. Leave the glue to dry overnight then use ordinary tile grout and spread it over the tiles with a spreader. Wipe away the excess with a damp cloth before it sets.

Step 9

You can glue the tiles as a complete panel to the wall of your dolls house above a washbasin, bath or sink. The little washbasin in the photograph is a project from "Making Doll's House Miniatures with Polymer Clay" by Sue Heaser.

Polychrome Tiles

The polychrome (multi-coloured) tiles using the second pattern sheet.

OIL LAMPS

These little oil lamps are great fun to make. Polymer clay is the material used for the shades, base and structure, while a pretty bead of any kind can be used for the body of the lamp. The tricky bit (as with any handmade miniature that needs to be symmetrical or perfectly straight) is to get the lamp to stand completely upright. This is solved by assembling the whole lamp on a central wire.

Expertise level: beginners to intermediate

Each lamp is approximately 6 cms (2 5/8 in) high including the acetate chimney

TOOLS AND MATERIALS

- Polymer Clay - Black and translucent - about 1/2 a 56g (2oz) block of each
- Circle cutters - 40mm (1 1/2 in), 25mm (1 in), 20mm (3/4 in),13mm (1/2 in), 10mm (3/8 in), 6mm (1/4 in) (see Cutters on page 76)
- Flower or heart cutter - 5mm (3/16 in)
- Two marbles, 25mm (1 in) diameter (or roll balls of polymer clay to this diameter, bake and cover tightly with aluminium foil.)
- Superglue
- Wire cutters or cutting pliers
- Gold acrylic paint or gold powder
- Acrylic varnish or polymer clay varnish

- Gold coloured wire, about 1mm (18ga.) thick (available from bead shops)
- Large decorated glass or ceramic bead, about 15mm (5/8 in) diameter
- Gold coloured headpin (from bead shops)
- Sandpaper
- Piece of thin acetate 25mm x 40mm (1 in x 1/12 in). This can be cut from the window of a packaging box. Alternatively, use a transparent brush protector that is sold protecting the bristles of a paintbrush – it should be about 7mm (5/16 in) diameter

Step 1

THE LAMP BASE

Roll out the black clay into a sheet 1.5mm (1/16 in) thick and lay the sheet on a tile. Cut out a circle 13mm (1/2 in) diameter and another of 10mm (3/8 in) diameter with the cutters. Remove the waste clay from around the circles.

Step 2

Slice under the small circle with your blade to free it from the tile and place it centrally on top of the larger circle, pressing it down lightly to join them together. Indent the centre of the base with a pencil end. Use a darning needle to make a hole in the centre of the base.

Step 3

Brush the base with gold powder and leave on the tile to bake. (If you are using gold paint, this should be applied when the pieces are baked.)

Step 4

Form a 10mm (3/8 in) ball of black clay and roll one side to shape it into a teardrop. Pierce lengthwise through the teardrop with the darning needle and brush with gold powder.

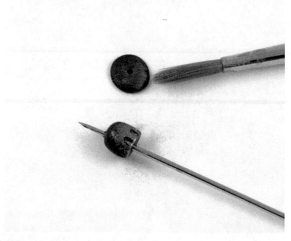

Step 5

Form a 3mm (1/8 in) ball of black clay and press onto the tile to make a disc about 5mm (3/16 in) across. Pierce the centre of the disc with the needle.

Form a 10mm ball of clay and shape into a short log. Cut this in half and use one half for the lamp burner. Indent round the top of the cut edge with the eye of a needle to suggest a burner. Pierce through the centre of the piece with the needle and press lightly down onto the tile to flatten the bottom. Pierce again into the side of the burner to make a hole for the wick adjuster.

Step 6

Brush the disc and the burner with gold powder and leave on the tile for baking.

Step 7

THE LAMPSHADE

Roll out a sheet of translucent polymer clay, 1mm (1/24 in) thick and cut out a circle with the 40mm (1 1/2 in) cutter. Steady one of the marbles on a tile with a piece of scrap clay. Mark the centre of the circle with a needle - this will help you cut out the centre after the next step.

Step 8

Place the circle of clay on top of the marble and coax the sides down round the marble by pressing opposite sides first and then working round, smoothing as you go.

When the clay is smoothed all round the marble, use a straight blade to trim the bottom edge straight.

Step 9

Use the 10mm (3/8 in) cutter to cut out a central circle in the middle of the applied clay, using the mark you made earlier to ensure that this is centrally placed. Repeat the last three steps to make a decorative top for the shade using smaller cutters: Apply a 20mm (3/4 in) disc of clay to the second marble and cut out the centre with the 10mm (3/8 in) cutter.

Step 10

Frill the edge of the shade top by pressing the point of a wool needle or similar blunt tool into the clay all round the edge. Leave the shade and the shade top on their marbles for baking.

Step 11

To make the shade support, roll out the black clay and cut out a circle with the 25mm (1 in) cutter. Use the tiny heart or flower cutter to cut out a pattern of holes. Pierce the centre of the support with the needle. The picture shows several examples with different designs.

Step 12

Brush the supports with gold powder and leave on the tile to bake.

Bake all the pieces (see Baking, p. 75) and leave until cool (they will not be fully hard until then). Remove from the tiles and marbles. Take care when removing the shade pieces from the marbles - they are usually firmly held on and you will need to slide the point of a needle round under the edges to free them before easing them off with your fingers.

Step 13

ASSEMBLY

This shows the pieces of the lamp before assembly.

Cut a length of wire about 6.5cm (2 1/2 in) long. Straighten it as much as you can. Cut the headpin to about 10mm (3/8 in) long. Thread the teardrop onto the wire, wide end downwards and apply glue to the base of the teardrop. Position the wire in the hole in the centre of the lamp base and push the teardrop down onto it to secure. The wire will ensure that the teardrop glues centrally to the base.

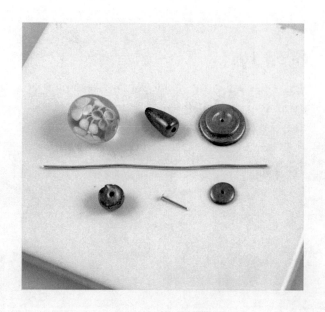

Step 14

Now thread on the glass bead and the small disc, then the lamp burner. Check that all are level and straight, then apply glue between each to hold them together. Glue the end of the headpin into the side hole in the burner.

Step 15

Thread the shade support onto the wire, gold side down. Check that it sits level, then glue in place. Trim the wire to 6mm (1/4 in) above the support and push the end over firmly to hold all the pieces on the wire. Trim again so the bent over part is about 3mm (1/8 in) long.

Step 16

Lay a piece of sandpaper on your work surface and rotate the bottom of the lampshade on it to smooth it and make it level. Repeat with the decorative top.

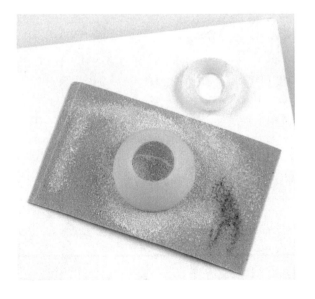

Step 17

Glue the bottom of the lampshade to the lampshade support and then glue the decorative top to the top of the shade.

Step 18

To make a glass chimney for the lamp, roll the piece of acetate round a paintbrush handle to make a tube 25mm (1 in) long and about 8mm (5/16 in) wide. Secure with transparent sticky tape. Glue this to the shade support inside the top of the shade. Finally varnish the shade to make it look glassy and over the gold powder to protect it.

FURTHER IDEAS

You can make a wonderful little collection of these oil lamps to decorate every room in a period dolls house. The lamp on the left has a square base cut out with square cutters and a straight lamp bottom made from a log of clay that has been rolled back and forth with a knitting needle to "groove" it. (See Grooving, p.20.) The lamp on the right has a "brass" base made from a large teardrop shaped in polymer clay and brushed with gold powder. You can also vary the decorative top of the lampshade.

For ideas on how to electrify polymer clay lamps, see Making Doll's House Miniatures with Polymer Clay by Sue Heaser.

LIBRARY GLOBE

Library Globes are models of the earth mounted on a pedestal so that they can spin and be used as a realistic map of the world. They have been in existence for many centuries and antique ones can fetch vast sums at auction. This 1:12 scale version is based on a table tennis ball, which is 1 1/2 in diameter (40mm) or an 18 inch globe at full scale. It would look delightful in a period dolls house - perhaps next to a desk in a library, or beside a bookcase.

Expertise level: beginner to intermediate
The Globe is about 8 cms (3 1/8 in) high

TOOLS AND MATERIALS

- Map – printed and cut out (see following page)
- Globe holder template traced and cut out.
- A standard size (40mm diameter) table tennis ball (available from sports shops)
- Sharp scissors
- PVA glue or Tacky glue and paintbrush
- Brown acrylic paint for antiquing the globe
- Acrylic varnish or polymer clay varnish
- Polymer Clay - Dark brown, light brown, gold - about 1/4 of a 56g (2 oz) block of each.
- 2mm drill bit and pin vice or small hand drill
- Wire cutters or cutting pliers
- Wire, 7.5cm (3in) long and about 1mm (18 ga.) thick
- Superglue

GLOBE MAP IMAGE

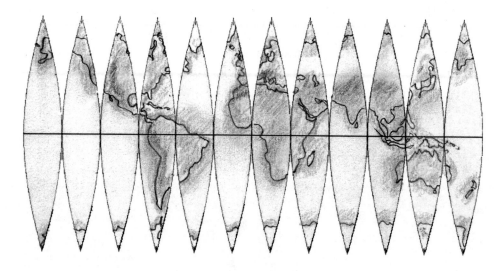

Equator line should = 12.5cms for correct scale

GLOBE HOLDER TEMPLATE

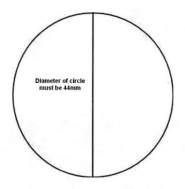

Diameter of circle
must be 44mm

Photocopy the map and the globe template and print them out at exactly the same size as indicated. Alternatively you can download the images from www.sueheaser.com and print them out from your computer (see instructions on page 5.)

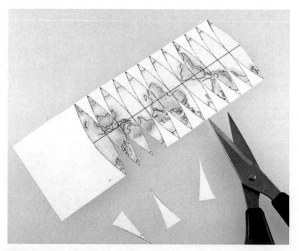

Step 1

THE GLOBE

Use sharp scissors to cut out the map accurately. It is best to cut just inside the lines so that any slight inaccuracies will show less when the map is glued to the table tennis ball.

Step 2

Hold the ball up to a light source - it should be slightly translucent. You will be able to see the central join so mark the position of this all the way round the ball to give the equator.

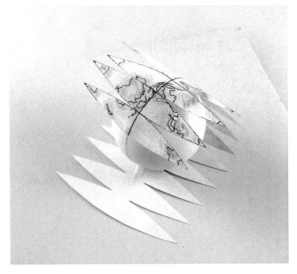

Step 3

Use the brush to apply PVA glue over the back of the cut-out map along the equator line and carefully press the map to the ball, matching the equator lines. Wrap the map right round the ball at this point. It should fit exactly because standard table tennis balls are all the same size.

Step 4

Now paint more glue over the inside of the pointed flaps of the map (called the gores) and press these carefully round the ball so that they all come to the same point (or the pole) on each side. You will need to smooth the paper into place and roll a paintbrush handle over any bubbles or protrusions to get it as snug as possible on the ball.

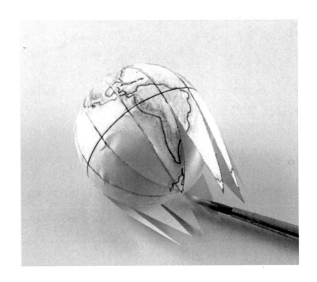

Step 5

Dilute some brown acrylic paint with water and brush a wash all over the map. This will brown it to look antique and also, as it dries, shrink the paper round the ball more tightly. Leave to dry fully, then varnish with acrylic varnish and leave to dry again.

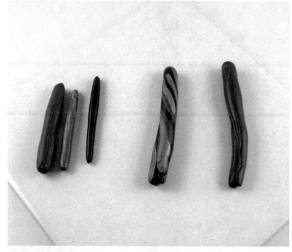

Step 6

THE STAND

To simulate wood grain, form a 20mm (3/4 in) ball of light brown polymer clay and a 10mm (3/8 in) ball each of the dark brown and gold clay. Form each ball into a log about 25mm (2in) long. Roll these together and then fold the resulting log in half and roll again. Repeat until the log has become well streaked to simulate wood. Do not continue too long or all the colours will merge into one. The finished marbled log should be 10mm (3/8 in) thick. Cut off a 13mm (1/2 in) length for the pedestal.

Step 7

GROOVING

Pierce the log lengthwise with a large darning needle. Roll it on a tile to lengthen the log to about 35mm (1 1/4 in) long and 5mm (3/16 in) thick. Now use a thick needle to roll the log back and forth on the tile. This will form a groove at that point and suggest turned wood. Repeat to make more grooves and try using different thickness of needle to vary the turned effect. Leave on the needle to bake.

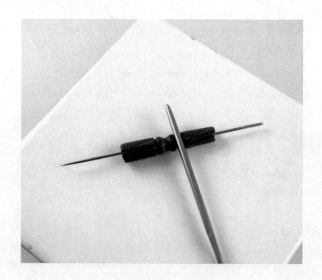

Step 8

Form a 10mm (3/8 in) ball and a 6mm (1/4 in) ball from the remaining marbled log. Press both down onto a tile to form two different sizes of disc, the larger one should be about 20mm (3/4 in) diameter and the smaller one about 13mm (1/2 in). Press the small one onto the larger one and indent the centre with the rubber on the end of a pencil or similar rounded tool.

Step 9

Roll the remaining wood effect log on a tile until it is 10cm (4in) long and then roll the log flat with your rolling pin to make a strip about 8mm (5/16 in) wide.

Use your long straight blade to trim the strip to 5mm (3/16 in) wide. This strip will form the holder for the globe.

Step 10

Use a dab of PVA glue to attach the circle template to a tile. Press the clay strip onto the tile just outside the template and curve it round the template evenly, pressing it down lightly to hold it in place. This ensures that the holder has the correct internal curve to hold the globe. Trim along the lines at the top and the bottom and leave on the tile to bake.

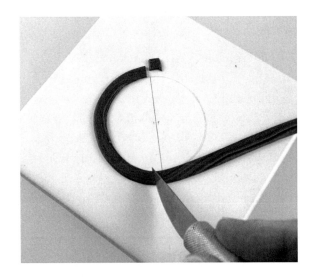

Step 11

Form a log of gold clay, 3mm (1/8 in) thick and cut two lengths of 5mm (3/16 in). Pierce one end of each with a needle to make the two finials for the globe holder.

Bake all the pieces and allow them to cool (see Baking on page 75).

Step 12

Drill a hole in the top and bottom of the globe, positioning the holes at the two poles. The ball should be fairly easy to drill as the walls are very thin.

Step 13

Use superglue to glue one end of the wire into a finial. Push the wire through the holes in the globe and trim the end to 5mm (3/16 in). Glue on the other finial. Hold the globe holder against the finials to check the fit. The globe should be held a few millimetres away from the holder and turn freely on the wire. Trim if necessary and then glue the finials to the ends of the globe holder.

Step 14

Pull the baked clay pedestal off the needle - if it is stuck, you may need to hold the needle with pliers and twist while you remove the pedestal. Trim the ends of the pedestal neatly - it should be about 25mm (1 in) long. Cut a slot with your craft knife in one end, wide enough to take the globe holder.

Step 15

Use superglue to glue the pedestal to the base ensuring that it is vertical. Now glue the globe holder into the slot on the pedestal. It should sit at an angle of 23.5° from the vertical but an approximation will do if you are not too fussy! Now your globe is ready to display. You may want to attach it to the floor or desk with tacky wax or similar so that it can be spun without toppling.

The Finished Globe which can be spun in its holder.

PICNIC BASKET

Polymer clay makes very convincing miniature baskets. Strips of cane-coloured clay are twisted to simulate basket cane and coiled over a former to make baskets of all shapes and sizes. Each clay coil can simply be pushed against the one below to secure it and build up the basket - no glue is needed.

This project shows how to make a traditional wicker picnic basket or hamper with a hinged lid and pretty fabric lining. The following project shows how to make the plates, knives and forks as well as the food to fill the basket.

Expertise level: Varied. Most beginners should manage the basket making techniques but the handles and fastenings are a bit fiddly.

The finished basket is about 55mm (2 1/4 in) long.

TOOLS AND MATERIALS

- Polymer Clay – Ochre, gold or light brown: 1 x 56g block; dark brown: small piece
- Small matchbox - approximately 5 x 3.5 x 1.5cm (2 x 1 3/8 x 5/8 inches)
- Kitchen foil
- Rolling strips (thick card or plastic), 2mm (1/12 in) thick and 1mm (1/24 in) thick
- Beading wire or any fine wire

- Fine brown cord or thick sewing thread - 5cm (2in) long
- Tacky glue
- Superglue
- Fine fabric - plain or with a small check or pattern. About 15cm x 10cm (6in x 4in)
- Pencil

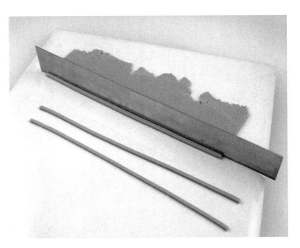

Step 1

THE BASKET LID

Lay the matchbox on a piece of foil and wrap it up neatly as though it was a parcel. This will be the former on which you will make the basket. There is no need to tape the ends. The foil will prevent the clay from sticking to the matchbox.

Step 2

Roll out the ochre clay between two rolling strips to make an even sheet 2mm (1/12 in) thick. Use your straight blade to cut long strips about 2mm (1/12 in) wide.

Step 3

Twist one of the strips to make a simulated basket cane and starting with a line in the centre, press down lightly onto the top of the wrapped matchbox in a spiral. The spiral should be oblong as shown so that as you add to it, the distance to the edge of the matchbox is the same all round. Press each new coil against the previous one to make the basket strong.

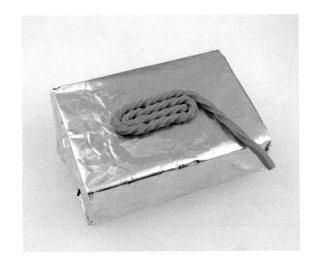

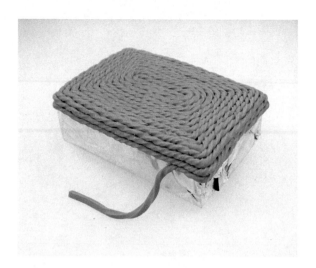

Step 4

When you reach the end of the first strip, trim the end at an angle. Trim the beginning of the next strip at the same angle and press the two together to make the join as invisible as possible. Continue adding more twisted strips until the top of the box is covered. You will need to pinch the corners of the rectangle to accentuate them as you go. When you reach the edges of the box top, adjust the strips by trimming or adding small pieces to cover the whole top.

Step 5

Now work down the sides of the box and finish with a neat row about 8mm (5/16 in) down. Use your blade to push the last strip straight all round. Make two holes with your needle for the wire hinges, one strip up from the bottom edge and 15mm (5/8 in) from each corner. Bake the matchbox with the woven basket lid on it for 30 minutes (see Baking on page 75). When it is cool, ease the basket off the matchbox. You should be able to flex the matchbox slightly inside the basket to remove it without damaging the basket.

Step 6

THE BASKET BASE

Roll out a sheet of clay 2mm (1/12 in) thick and lay it on a tile. Place the matchbox on the clay sheet and cut all round with your blade to make the basket bottom.

Step 7

Now apply strips as before, starting at the bottom and press the first coil against the edges of the sheet of clay. Continue until you are almost at the top of the box as shown. Make two holes in the top of the basket base, each 15mm (5/8 in) from the corners and one strip below the edge. These should match the holes made in the basket lid for the wire hinges. Bake the base as for the top and remove from the matchbox.

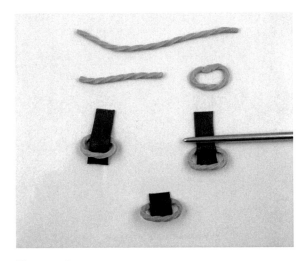

Step 8

THE HANDLES

Cut a strip of ochre clay, a little thinner than the ones for the main basket and twist. Cut two lengths of 25mm (1 in) from the twisted strip and coax each into a ring, pressing the ends together and pressing this join down on a tile to hold it steady. Roll a small sheet of dark brown clay, about 1mm (1/24 in) thick and cut two strips, each 5mm (3/16 in) wide and 10mm (3/8 in) long. Push one of these through each ring (you can lift the lower side of the ring to make this easier. Use a wool needle to press the brown strip down onto the tile on either side of the join in the ring. Trim the excess clay. Bake the two handles on the tile for 20 minutes.

Step 9

THE HINGES

Thread a length of fine wire through each pair of corresponding holes in the basket lid and base. Twist until they are fairly tight but there is still free movement. Trim the twisted ends fairly short and push them down into the base of the basket against the back.

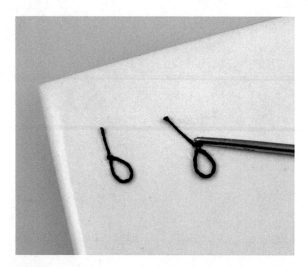 

Step 10

CATCHES AND HANDLES

Cut the brown cord into two 25mm (1 in) lengths and curve each into a loop as shown. Hold in place with a dab of tacky glue and leave to dry.

Step 11

Form a small log of dark brown clay, 3mm (1/8 in) thick and cut two 3mm (1/8 in) lengths for toggles. Bake for 10 minutes. Superglue one end of each toggle to the front of the basket, one strip down from the top edge of the base and evenly spaced about 25mm (1 in) apart. Mark their positions with a pencil on the basket lid.

Step 12

Trim the cord loops and glue with tacky glue to the inside front of the lid at the points marked. Make sure they are long enough to go over the toggles when the basket lid is closed. The pencil marks can be removed with a soft eraser.

Step 13

Use superglue to glue a basket handle to the centre of each of the two sides.

Step 14

Stand the basket on the reverse of the fabric and draw round with a pencil, leaving a 6mm (1/4 in) border all round. Cut out the rectangle and use this as a pattern to cut out a second rectangle the same size.

Step 15

Use tacky glue to glue a hem all round a fabric rectangle, measuring the size against the basket to ensure it will fit inside the lid. Glue the hemmed rectangle inside the lid, raw edges down, and repeat with the second rectangle for the bottom of the basket.

Step 16

Finally glue two pieces of soutache braid from the inside of the lid to the inside base of the basket on each side, making them just long enough so that the lid sits open in a vertical position.

The basket is now ready to be filled with goodies for a picnic!

PICNIC BASKET CONTENTS

This project shows how to make the knives, forks and plates to go in the picnic basket as well as some delicious traditional British picnic goodies.

Expertise Level: The food is easy for beginners; the plates and cutlery are intermediate.

TOOLS AND MATERIALS

- Polymer Clay – small quantities (less than 1/4 of a 56g (2oz) block) of white, navy blue, beige, golden yellow, red, ochre, medium brown
- Rolling strips - 1mm (1/24 in) thick pieces of card
- Round cutter - 13mm (1/2 in) diameter
- Square cutter - 10mm (3/8 in) - or cut by hand
- Large marker pen (or use a knife handle or cosmetic tube) with a flat end - 10mm (3/8 in) diameter is ideal
- Talcum powder
- Pearl Ex Silver powder (or paint with silver acrylic paint after baking)
- Acrylic gloss varnish
- Cream paper
- Tweezers
- Tacky glue
- Sandpaper
- Ground rice, semolina or cornmeal
- Sesame seeds
- Black marker pen or black paint

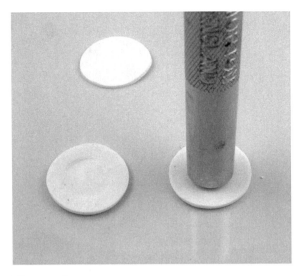

Step 1

THE PLATES

You will need 2 for the basket and several more for serving the food.

Roll out the white clay between the rolling strips to make a sheet 1mm (1/24 in) thick. Cut out four circles with the circle cutter.

Step 2

Dust the tile with talc and lay a cut-out circle on it, flipping it over so that the cut edge looks thinner and avoids the bevelled edge caused by the cutter. Smear some talc over the top of the circle and place the pen end as exactly in the centre of the circle as you can. Press firmly to indent the centre of the plate - the edge should rise slightly all round to make a plate shape. Repeat for the other plates and then bake. Varnish when cool.

Step 3

THE THERMOS FLASK

Roll a log of navy blue clay, 10mm (3/8 in) thick and place in the freezer for 10 minutes to harden so it will not distort when cut. Trim to 20mm (3/4 in). Make a 13mm (1/2 in) ball of white clay and roll lightly until it becomes a short log, the same thickness as the navy blue log and with rounded ends. Chill in the freezer and cut off one end for the thermos cup, about 10mm (3/8 in) from one rounded end. Press on to the top of the navy log.

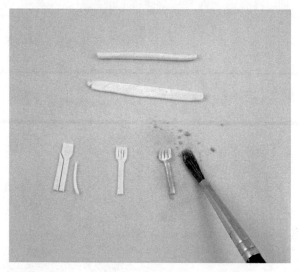

Step 4

Roll a thin log of white clay and apply all
round the join between the white and navy
clay to neaten it. Roll another of navy blue
and apply round the bottom of the thermos.
Form a 1mm (1/24 in) log of white and flatten
it slightly for the handle. Cut a length, 10mm
(3/8 in) long and apply one end to the bottom
of the thermos cup. Curve the other end
upwards and press on about 2/3rds of the way
up the cup. Remember that the cup on top of a
flask has to be upside-down! Trim the end and
then bake the flask.

Step 5

THE CUTLERY

Roll a 1.5mm (1/16 in) thick log of white clay
and roll flat with your roller to make a strip
about 3mm (1/8 in) wide. Cut the strip into
several 15mm (5/8 in) lengths. (It is easier to
make plenty and use the best!) Press the
strips down on the tile to keep them still while
you work on them and cut each into a fork
shape, removing the scrap clay. Make three
cuts in the wide end of each, slice under the
resulting prongs and lift them up a little to
give the forks shape. Brush all over with
silver powder.

Step 6

Form a 10mm (3/8 in) log of white clay and
flatten on a tile until it is 3mm (1/8 in) thick.
Press the side of a pencil into the clay along
one edge as shown to make a knife-shaped
cross section with a tang.

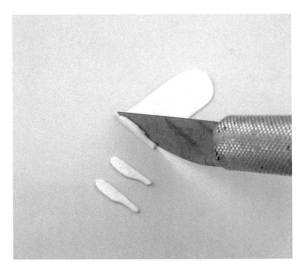

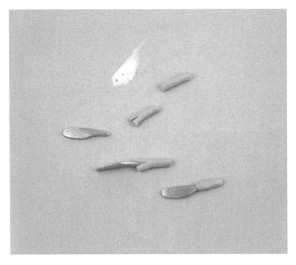

Step 7

Freeze the shaped log to make it firm and then cut slices for the knife blades and brush all over with silver powder. Bake with the forks.

Step 8

Form a 2mm (1/12 in) thick log of beige clay and cut several 10mm (3/8 in) lengths for the knife handles. Cut a slit in one end of each. Smear glue on the tang end of a baked knife blade and push it into the slit in the end of a handle, squeezing the clay round to secure. Repeat for the remaining knives and bake.

Step 9

MUGS

Form a 6mm (1/4 in) log of white clay and cut several 5mm (3/16 in) lengths. Pierce about half way into the end of one length with the wool needle.

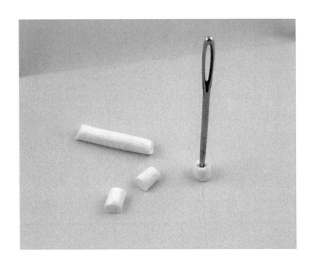

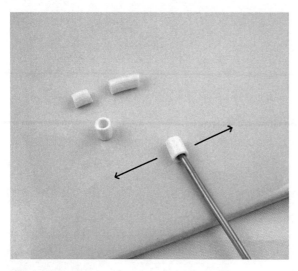

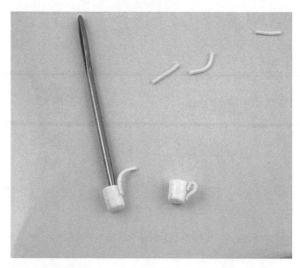

Step 10

With the clay log on the needle, push the
needle from side to side on the edge of a tile so
that the log rotates and the hole enlarges to
make a little mug.

Step 11

Roll a 1mm (1/24 in) thick log of white for the
handles. Cut a 10mm (3/8 in) length and apply
for the handle as shown. Repeat to make more
mugs. Bake and after baking, paint with a
small design if you wish. Varnish with gloss
varnish.

Step 12

DISPLAYING THE CUTLERY AND PLATES

Cut strips of paper about 1.5mm (1/16 in)
thick. Glue two plates together and glue two
strips of paper in a cross over them and round
the back. Glue the plates to the centre of the
inside of the picnic basket lid. Glue the forks
and knives on either side of the plates using
tweezers to position them.

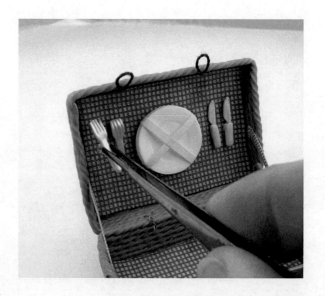

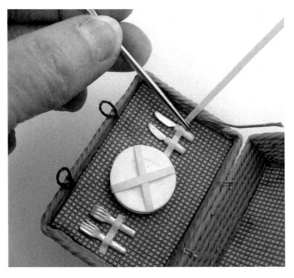

Step 13

Glue a strip of paper across the handles of each pair, pushing it down between them and trimming it to fit.

Step 14

SANDWICHES

Roll a 1mm (1/24 in) thick sheet of beige clay and press all over with sandpaper to texture it. Cut 10mm (3/8 in) squares by hand or with a cutter and cut each square in half diagonally. Flip one triangle over and lay on thin slices of golden yellow (cheese) and red (tomato). Press on another triangle, textured side up. Try using different colours to suggest different fillings. Bake the sandwiches.

Step 15

HAM AND EGG PIE

Roll a 2mm (1/12 in) thick log of golden yellow and wrap it in a 1mm (1/24 in) sheet of white to make the egg. Trim to 20mm (3/4 in) long and bake.

Step 16

Mix together a 20mm (3/4 in) ball of beige clay and a little red to make a ham pink. Roll this into a sheet and sprinkle with ground rice. Fold up the sheet of clay and roll and fold again to incorporate the ground rice into the clay. Continue adding ground rice in the same way until you have a nicely textured ball of clay when cut open.

Step 17

Mould the pink textured clay round the baked egg centre and shape into a loaf shape about 20mm (3/4 in) long and 10mm (3/8 in) thick. Roll the ochre clay into a sheet, 1mm (1/24 in) thick. Use this to wrap the pink loaf.

Step 18

Crimp round the edge with the point of the wool needle and make slits in the top. Bake and when still warm, cut a few slices.

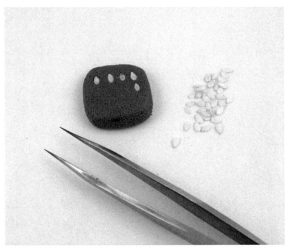

Step 19

GINGERBREAD

Mix ground rice into a 20mm (3/4 in) ball of caramel brown clay in the same way as for the ham and egg pie. Shape into a square cake, about 20mm (3/4 in) across. Press sesame seeds for almonds on to the top of the cake in a pattern using the tweezers. Bake and cut a few chunks when still warm.

Step 20

BANANAS

Form four or five 6mm (1/4 in) balls of golden yellow clay and shape each into a short log with pointed ends. Press together into a bunch. Use a marker pen to make lines of black down the sides of the bananas. Bake.

Display the picnic basket with the food arranged on plates or in small squares of paper as though it has just been unwrapped.

The finished basket with all its contents and picnic food.

GRANDFATHER CLOCK

I have always loved grandfather clocks and we have a battered old 18th century clock in our hall. Granddad, as I call him, is rather unpredictable and his time keeping is a bit doddery... but he really is one of the family.

So here is a grandfather clock to grace the hall or parlour of your dolls house. Polymer clay simulates mahogany to perfection - it is finer grained than the finest woodgrain so appears beautifully in scale. The clock parts are cut from sheets of clay, then baked and assembled and the project is fairly easy even if you have not done much with polymer clay before.

The face is reproduced from an antique clock made by Richard Francis of Attleborough in Norfolk, UK - dated about 1790. I am grateful to Vernon Morris of Hythe in Kent for supplying the photograph of the lovely painted clock face.

Expertise level: Beginner to intermediate – take care when cutting out the pieces and gluing them together – they need to be precise.

The finished clock is about 13 cms (5 1/8 in) tall.

TOOLS AND MATERIALS

- Clock templates printed or traced and cut out
- Clock faceprinted and cut out
- Polymer Clay, 56g (2oz) blocks: dark brown x 1, black x 1, gold x 1/2
- Knitting needle - about 2-3mm thick
- Ruler

- 2mm (1/12 in) thick rolling strips (Or use a pasta machine set to roll sheets about 2mm thick)
- Superglue (see Gluing, p. 75)
- Small piece of fine gold coloured wire for a key

TEMPLATES AND CLOCK FACE

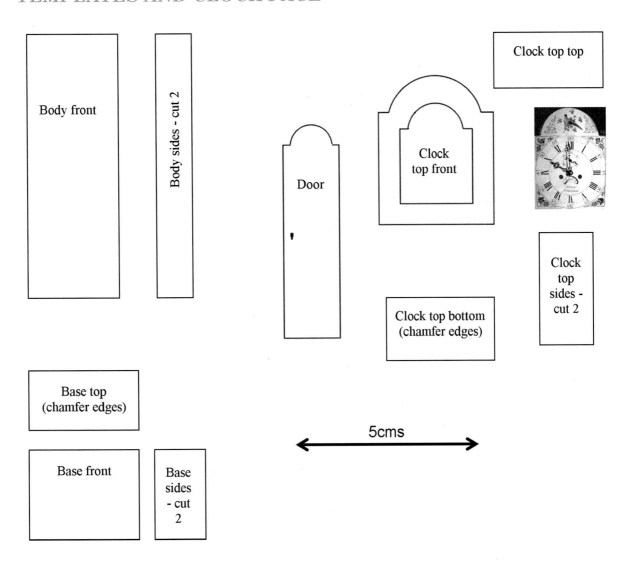

Body front

Body sides - cut 2

Door

Clock top front

Clock top top

Clock top sides - cut 2

Clock top bottom (chamfer edges)

Base top (chamfer edges)

Base front

Base sides - cut 2

5cms

Photocopy the page and print at exactly the size indicated. Alternatively you can download the images from www.sueheaser.com and print them out from your computer (see instructions on page 5.)

Step 1

To mix a simulated mahogany wood grain, take 1/4 block each of the dark brown and black clays and 1/8 block of the gold clay. Roll each of the colours into a log of the same length, press together and roll into a single log.

Step 2

Fold the log in half, aligning the stripes of colour, and roll again to lengthen. Continue rolling and folding until the log has fine streaks of colour that look like miniature wood grain.

Step 3

Roll the log out between the 2mm (1/12 in) rolling strips to make a sheet (or use a pasta machine). Try to keep the streaks running straight all down the sheet. Repeat to make more wood grain sheet as required. It is easier to make in small batches like this rather than one large sheet.

Step 4

Place the sheet on a tile and lay on the cut-out templates for the clock base (front and sides), the clock body (front and sides) and the clock top (sides and top). Cut round each piece using a straight slicer blade and remove waste clay from around it. Do not attempt to remove the cut out pieces from the tile or they will distort. They will be baked on the tile and removed when cool.

Step 5

Now cut out the base top and the clock top bottom. You can use a thicker sheet for these pieces if you wish to make more of the chamfering of the edges. Press the side of a knitting needle on to the front and side edges of each piece to chamfer it.

Step 6

Cut out the clock top front, using a pointed blade to cut round the curve at the top of the clock and to cut away the central area for the clock face. Remove the waste clay as before.

Step 7

To make the moulding round the top of the clock, cut a strip of clay from the clay sheet, 5cms (2 in) long and 3mm (1/8 in) wide. Press the edge of a ruler onto it to make a groove all along the strip.

Step 8

Press the moulding round the top of the clock and trim to fit. Cut two more short pieces, the cuts angled as shown, to apply on either side. Press another length of moulding along the bottom of the clock top.

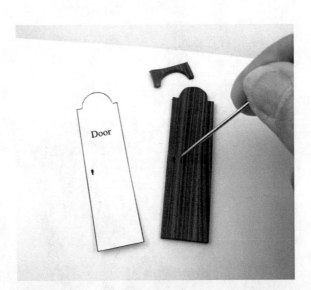

Step 9

Cut out the door for the front of the clock body and make a small hole with a needle to suggest a key hole. Bake all pieces on the tiles and remove when cool.

Step 10

Glue the base sides to the base front, ensuring that they are at right angles to the front. Glue on the base top. Glue the body sides to the body front.

Step 11

Glue the cut out paper clock face to the back of the clock top front ensuring that it fits in the opening. Glue the top sides to the clock front. The top bottom should be glued to the clock top as shown - with the chamfered edge downwards. Finally glue on the top of the clock top.

Step 12

Glue the door to the front of the clock and then assemble the clock by gluing the top and base to the body.

Step 13

To strengthen the clock, make it a back. Press the whole piece on a rolled out sheet of mahogany clay which has been placed on a tile. Cut round the clock with a knife and remove the waste clay. Bake the clock back on the tile and then glue it to the back of the clock. Finally bend the gold wire into a tiny key shape and glue into the key hole.

MINIATURE THEATRE

There is something particularly delightful about a miniature theatre and this little theatre is at the correct scale for a 1:12 toy theatre – in other words, a toy theatre for a dolls house. The play being performed is "A Midsummer Night's Dream" by William Shakespeare and in the scene shown, Titania is being wooed by Bottom, complete with his ass's head while Puck looks on. Miniature theatres have been popular for centuries and examples can be found all over Europe. They are not just made as toys and there are many examples that are for adult enjoyment with elaborate plays and scenery being created.

Polymer clay is an ideal material for making a sturdy little theatre while printed paper and card is used for the scenery. The tiny actors are made in polymer clay and glued onto rods so they can be moved about the stage.

Expertise level: Theatre construction is suitable for beginners. The tiny actors are a little more challenging because of their size.

Height of Miniature Theatre: 8.5 cms (3 5/8 in).

TOOLS AND MATERIALS

- Polymer Clay 56g (2oz) blocks: dark brown x1; white x 1; small amounts of black, flesh, crimson, yellow, grey
- Rolling strips, 3mm (1/8 in) thick (use two pieces of thick cardboard)
- Set square
- Sheet of thin card
- Small sharp scissors
- Scalpel (optional)
- Superglue - use to glue the baked polymer clay pieces of the theatre together
- Tacky glue or UHU glue - use to glue paper, card, ribbon and braid to baked polymer clay
- 25cms (10 in) of 10mm (3/8 in) wide ribbon for the theatre base - choose a suitable colour or pattern
- 20cms (8in) of 3mm (1/8 in) wide patterned or plain ribbon to decorate the proscenium

TEMPLATES, THEATRE TOP AND SCENERY

Photocopy this page and print out at exactly the size indicated. Alternatively you can download the images from www.sueheaser.com and print them out from your computer (see instructions on page 5.)

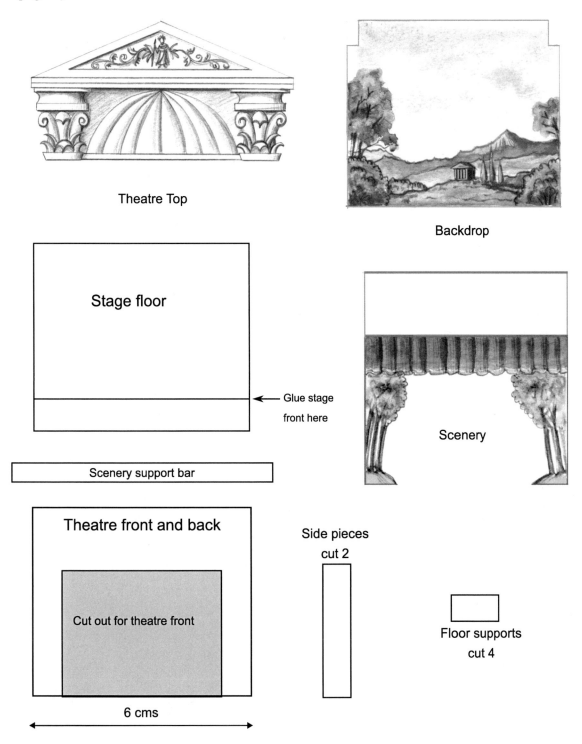

Theatre Top

Backdrop

Stage floor

← Glue stage front here

Scenery support bar

Scenery

Theatre front and back

Cut out for theatre front

6 cms

Side pieces
cut 2

Floor supports
cut 4

THE THEATRE
Step 1

Cut out the theatre templates. Roll out the dark brown clay between the rolling strips to make an even sheet 3mm (1/8 in) thick. Lay this on a tile and place the theatre floor and floor supports templates on top.

Step 2

Cut round the templates using a straight blade or craft knife and pull away the scrap clay. Do not remove the pieces from the tile - they will be removed after baking to avoid distortion.

Step 3

Roll out the white clay in the same way and place on a second tile. Cut out the front and back of the theatre, the side pieces and the scenery support bar. Bake all the pieces on their tiles for 30 minutes to ensure they are as strong as possible. Leave to cool and remove from the tile. They will be slightly flexible when cool.

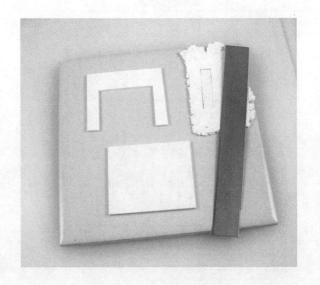

Step 4

Use superglue to glue the white theatre back to the back edge of the floor, ensuring that it stands upright by holding the edge of a set square or piece of stiff card against it. Lay the side pieces on the stage in front of the theatre back to measure the exact position to glue the theatre front to the floor. Glue in place and then glue the side pieces in place between the top of the theatre back and front.

Step 5

Glue the four floor supports in place under the floor - two at the front and two at the back as shown.

Step 6

Glue the thinner ribbon in two lengths to the theatre front on either side of the proscenium. Glue another length to the front of the theatre across the top of the proscenium arch.

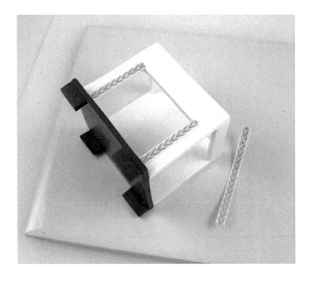

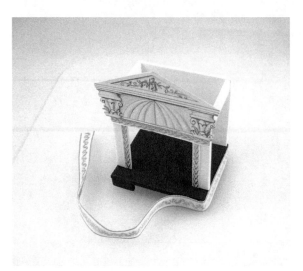

Step 7

Glue the printed paper theatre top to a piece of card and cut it out, using sharp scissors or a scalpel to cut round the edges. Glue the theatre top to the front of the theatre above the ribbon.

Step 8

Glue the wider ribbon all round the bottom of the theatre to cover the floor supports, placing the join at the back.

THE BACKDROP AND SCENERY
Step 9

Cut out the theatre backdrop. Glue the front scenery to thin card and then cut it out, using a scalpel or sharp scissors to cut round the trees and curtain. Glue one long edge of the scenery support bar to the top of the scenery, ensuring that when the bar rests on the theatre side pieces, the bottoms of the trees just touch the stage floor.

Step 10

Glue the backdrop in place on the back of the theatre, adjusting the notches so that it fits and lies flat. Hang the front scenery on the theatre side pieces - you can glue it in place here if you wish.

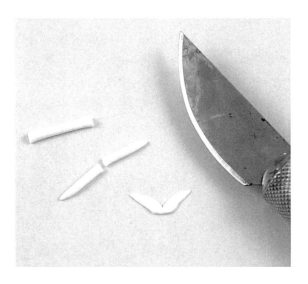

THE ACTORS
Step 11

These are made in relief working on a tile. At this scale, each figure should be about 13mm (1/2 in) tall. They are glued to baked strips of clay so that they can be moved around the stage from the sides of the theatre.

TITANIA: Roll a thin log of white clay, about 2mm (1/12 in) thick and 13mm (1/2 in) long. Point both ends and cut in half for two wings. Press these down onto a tile, splayed out as shown.

Step 12

Form a 3mm (1/8 in) ball of white clay and shape into a cone. Press down onto the wings for the dress. Mark lines on the dress to suggest folds and indent the bottom edge to suggest a frill. Roll a 1mm (1/24 in) thick log and cut two 3mm (1/8 in) lengths for the arms. Point one end of each and press the pointed end onto the top of the dress. Roll a 1mm (1/24 in) thick log of flesh clay. Cut thin slices with your knife and apply to the end of each arm for hands.

Step 13

Form a 1.5mm (1/16 in) ball of flesh clay and press on to the top of the dress for the head, over the tops of the arms. Roll out a very thin sheet of dark brown clay and cut thin strips with your knife - applying them with the knife to the head for hair and trailing them down.

Step 14

Finally use a pin to make tiny holes in the face for eyes and mouth and apply some tiny slices of white clay to the head for a tiara.

Step15

BOTTOM (WITH ASS'S HEAD):

Form a 2mm (1/12 in) thick log of grey clay, 6mm (1/4 in) long, and cut off one end to straighten it. Press on to a tile and curve the rounded end round into a donkey's head. Flatten a 1mm (1/24 in) log of grey on the tile and cut two slices for ears, applying them with your knife to the top of the head.

Make a cone of crimson clay as for Titania's dress above and apply arms in the same way, trimming it shorter for a shirt.

Form a 2mm (1/12 in) thick log of black clay and cut a 5mm (3/16 in) length. Flatten onto the tile and mark a line in the centre to suggest two legs. Apply two slices of black to the bottom of the legs for the feet.

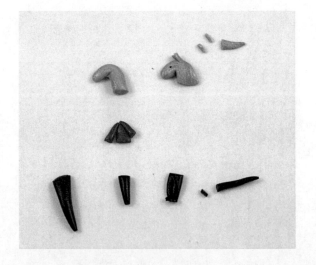

Step 16

Slide a blade under the donkey head and press it on to the top of the shirt. Press the legs against the bottom of the shirt. Apply hands as before. Apply small slices of yellow for buttons and pierce with a pin. Make an eye hole in the donkey head.

PUCK: Puck's body is made in the same way as Bottom's body but in leaf green and brown. His head is applied as Titania's and he has short brown hair. Try creating further actors for your theatre using the same techniques.

Close- up photograph of the actors. The tiny supporting block is just visible behind Bottom.

Step 17

Roll out some dark brown clay and cut thin strips, 3mm (1/8 in) wide and about 5cm (2in) long. Apply a small block of clay to the end of each to support the figure. Bake the actors and the strips on the tile and when cool, glue each figure to a strip as shown. Push the actors onto the stage from the wings (open sides) of the theatre.

The Theatre from the front showing the actors in position on the stage.

WOOD BURNER STOVE

Wood burning stoves were first developed in the Victorian age and were the result of enclosing fireplaces so that wood or coal burned more efficiently. The earlier stoves were usually made of cast iron which was often beautifully decorated with mouldings and embellishments. This miniature version is a typical wood burning stove of the mid to late 1800's and its design is still used today.

Polymer clay is particularly good at simulating metal and black polymer clay looks just like miniature cast iron. The component parts of the stove are all made first and then the stove is assembled. The only really tricky part is making the hinges so if you would rather make a simpler project, glue all the hinges to the stove front and glue the doors in place, either open or closed as you wish.

Wood burning stoves are timeless so this little stove looks equally good in a miniature Victorian cottage or a modern country dolls house.

Expertise level: Intermediate with glued hinges; Advanced with moving hinges.

Finished stove is approximately 6 cms (2 5/8 in) across and 5 cms (2 in) high excluding the stove pipe.

TOOLS AND MATERIALS

- Stove templates traced and cut out
- Polymer Clay - black - one 56g (2 oz) block
- Rolling guides – a pair of cardboard or plastic strips about 2mm (1/12 in) thick and another pair of 1mm (1/24 in) thick
- Two brass lace-making pins, or ordinary dressmakers' pin (brass pins are easier to cut)
- Super glue - or UHU glue
- Scrap of kitchen foil
- Wire cutters or cutting pliers
- Small pieces of acetate for the door windows. These can be cut from the clear acetate windows used in cardboard packaging.

NB: All pieces are made and baked on a tile. They should not be moved until after baking to avoid distortion.

TEMPLATES FOR THE STOVE

Photocopy this page and print out at exactly the size indicated. Alternatively you can download the images from www.sueheaser.com and print them out from your computer (see instructions on page 5.)

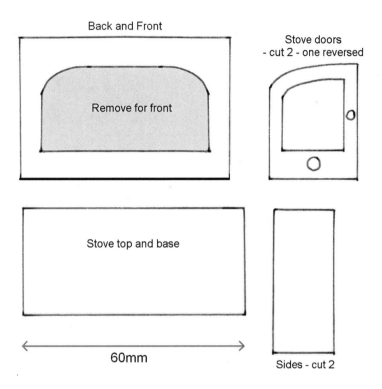

Back and Front

Remove for front

Stove doors
- cut 2 - one reversed

Stove top and base

60mm

Sides - cut 2

Step 1

THE STOVE BODY

Condition the polymer clay by working it in your hands until it is soft and pliable. Roll out the black clay between the 2mm (1/12 in) rolling strips to make an even sheet and lay this on a tile. Place the cut out templates on the clay and use a craft knife or slicer blade to cut out the back and two sides of the stove. Remove the waste clay from around the pieces and leave them on the tile for baking.

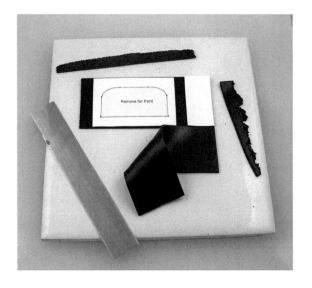

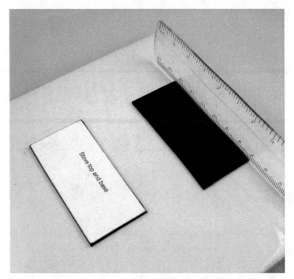

Step 2

Now cut out the stove top and base in the same way. Use the edge of a ruler to mark grooves just in from the edges all round to decorate them.

Step 3

Trim the corners off the stove top and base and smooth with your fingers to round them. Leave on the tile for baking as before.

Step 4

Cut out the stove front and then cut out the front opening with the point of your craft knife, taking care not to mark the surrounding clay. You will need to cut with the knife point carefully into all the corners and then use the knife blade to remove the waste clay from the centre.

Step 5

THE STOVE DOORS

Cut out the stove doors on a tile in the same way, reversing the template for the second door. Cut out and remove the clay from the window openings.

Step 6

Roll out more black clay 1mm (1/24 in) thick, and cut several 1mm (1/24 in) wide strips, about 25mm (1 in) long. Apply these to the window openings in a cross as shown, trimming them to fit inside the window opening. Match the two windows as much as possible and press the ends of the clay strips into the sides of the openings to secure them.

Step 7

For the front air vents, use a blunt needle to mark two slots on the bottom front of each door. Form a log of black clay, 2mm (1/12 in) thick and cut two lengths of the same measurement. Form these into little balls and press onto each slot for knobs. Impress the centre of each knob with a blunt needle to finish it. Repeat to make two more knobs for the doors.

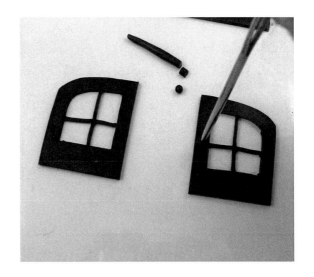

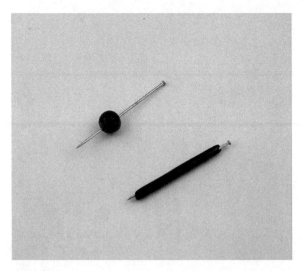

Step 8

Mark round the edge of each door with a blunt needle to decorate it and give it a cast iron effect.

Step 9

HINGES

Form two balls of black clay, about 6mm (1/4 in) diameter and pierce one with a pin. Roll the clay on a tile, with the pin horizontal inside, until it makes an even log with the pin through the middle. Repeat for the other clay ball and pin. Place on a tile for baking.

Step 10

THE GRATE

Roll out a 1mm (1/24 in) thick sheet and lay on a tile. Cut a rectangle, 65mm (2 1/2 in) long and about 25mm (1 in) wide. Cut three strips from the long edge, 2mm (1/12 in) wide and 65mm (2 1/2 in) long, and leave them on the tile for baking. The grate will be cut and assembled when baked.

Step 11

THE STOVE FEET

Roll out a thick sheet of clay, 5mm (3/16 in) thick, and lay on a tile. Cut into a strip 10mm (3/8 in) wide and about 40mm (1 1/2 in) long. Cut out four stove feet from this, making them each 6mm (1/4 in) wide and cut at an angle as shown.

Step 12

THE STOVE PIPE

Form a log of black clay 8mm (5/16 in) thick and as long as you need to reach the ceiling of your dolls house room, or up inside the fireplace. The easiest way to roll a really even log is to use a sheet of glass or Perspex as shown and roll back and forth. Trim the ends neatly. Lay a needle across the log, 10mm (3/8 in) from one end, and roll it back and forth to make a groove and suggest the bottom of a stove pipe. Bake all the pieces on the tiles.

Step 13

FIXED HINGES: For an easier project to give the stove fixed doors, just glue the hinges with their pins directly to the stove front and glue the doors to them, either open or shut as you wish. Continue from Step 18.

WORKING HINGES: This is delicate work - be careful not to let superglue flow where it should not go or the doors will not open properly. Remove the pins from the logs and cut each log into four 3mm (1/8 in) lengths. Keep each set of four lengths together - each set is used on one door and if you mix them up, you will not get such an accurate result.

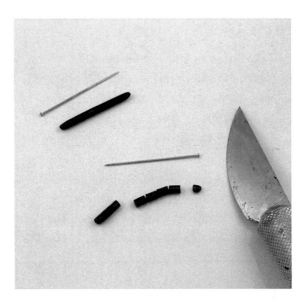

Step 14

Place the doors on the stove front so that you can position the hinges in the correct place. Thread two hinge lengths onto a pin and position them apart so that when the pin is laid next to the door, they are in the positions shown. Squeeze a small pool of superglue onto a piece of foil (it will stay wet for a reasonably long time) and use a cocktail stick to apply glue to the underside of each hinge piece. Press them down again onto the stove front, taking care that glue does not touch the door.

Step 15

Remove the pin and then push it through one of the remaining hinge pieces, then through the top glued piece, through the second remaining piece and finally the bottom glued piece. Push the free hinge pieces down onto the fixed pieces so they make two pairs.

Step 16

You now need to glue the door to the unattached top hinges pieces. Carefully apply glue to the door side of each top hinge piece of each pair and push the door against them, aligning it in the correct place on the front. Hold it until it sticks. The door should now open and shut on the hinges. Repeat for the other door, ensuring that it is aligned and snugly up against the first door when the hinges are glued to the stove front.

Step 17

Remove the pins and cut the point off each so that they match the hinges. Push each pin through each set of the hinges until the head rests on the upper hinge.

Step 18

THE GRATE

Roll out a sheet of black clay, 1mm (1/24 in) thick and cut a strip for the grate front, 50mm (2in) long and 6mm (1/4 in) wide. Lay on a tile. Cut two of the baked grate strips into 13mm (1/2 in) lengths and press them onto the soft grate front, spacing them evenly as shown, using a ruler to help you.

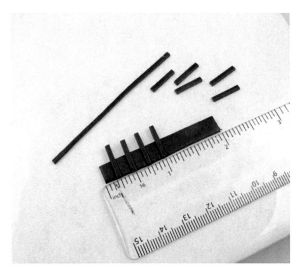

Step 19

Bake for 20 minutes and when cool, trim the uprights with a straight blade to straighten them and glue the remaining strip along the top, across all the uprights. Trim to 50mm (2in) wide.

Step 20

Glue the completed grate on the inside of the stove front as shown. The top needs to show through the doors from the front.

Step 21

Glue the stove sides to the back, ensuring that they are at 90° to the back. Glue the stove front to the stove sides.

Step 22

Glue the stove body to the stove base, positioning it so that it is at the back of the base with a ledge at the front. Glue on the stove top and glue the feet under the base.

Step 23

Glue the stove pipe to the top of the stove. Cut small pieces of acetate to fit inside the door windows and glue inside each door. Now put the dolls house kettle on and enjoy the stove! To suggest a fire burning in the stove, place some crinkled orange metallic paper inside.

VICTORIAN KITCHEN SCALES

Decorative cast iron scales are a favourite collectible from the Victorian kitchen. Here, polymer clay is formed into miniature scales that can be made to balance with the set of "brass" weights. Working miniatures are a delight to make and while this is a more advanced clay project, it is well worth the challenge.

Expertise level: Advanced

The Scales are approximately 3cms (1 1/4 in) high.

TOOLS AND MATERIALS

- Polymer Clay - Black: about 1/2 a 56g (2oz) block
- Pencil - round and smooth
- A brass lace-making pin, or ordinary dressmakers' pin (brass pins are easier to cut)
- Circle cutter - 25mm (1 in) - or draw a circle on card and cut out to use as a template
- Two large marbles, about 20mm (3/4 in) diameter
- Ball-headed pin or tool
- Superglue
- Wire cutters or cutting pliers
- Gold acrylic paint
- Acrylic varnish or polymer clay varnish
- Fine paintbrush

Step 1

Form a 15mm (5/8 in) ball of black clay and shape it into a short log about 25mm (1 in) long. Press a pencil into the centre of the log as shown and push it back and forth to roll the log and thin the centre into a waist.

Step 2

Press the dumbbell shape onto the board to flatten the base. Now pinch the tops of the two side pieces into points. Lay the scales base on its side and cut off the tips of the points to give two flat platforms.

Step 3

Form two 3mm (1/8 in) balls of clay and flatten onto the board to make two 6mm (1/4 in) wide disks. Press these lightly onto the tops of the two platforms.

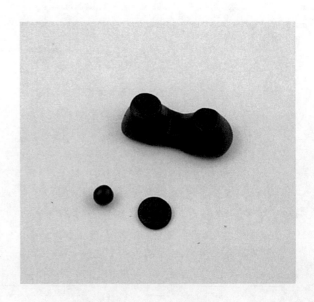

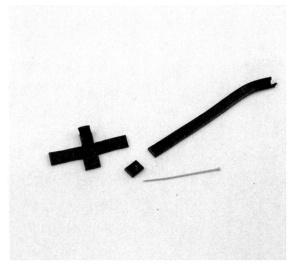

Step 4

Roll out a sheet of clay, 1.5mm (1/16 in) thick and use a slicer blade to cut a strip 5mm (3/16 in) wide and about 25mm (1 in) long (or long enough to reach across the two platforms) and two 5mm (3/15 in) squares. Apply the squares to the sides of the strip to make a cross.

Step 5

Cut two more squares and pierce both in the centre with a pin as shown. Press the bottom edges of the squares onto the short arms of the cross so they stand upright.

Step 6

To make the balancing bar, cut a rectangle of clay 25mm by 6mm (1 in by 1/4 in) from the 1.5mm (1/16 in) sheet and lay on a tile. Cut out the centre as shown leaving a frame at least 2mm (1/12 in) wide.

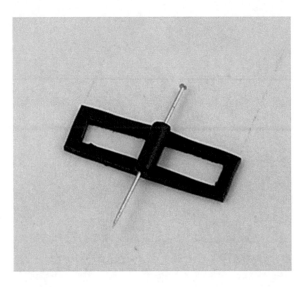

Step 7

Form a 3mm (1/8 in) log, trim to 8mm (5/16 in) long and pierce with a pin for the balance bar hinge. Now press the hinge, with the pin still through it, onto the centre of the cut out strip. (This will be the underside when assembled.) Leave on the tile with the pin in place for baking (removing it would distort it).

Step 8

Roll out a 1mm (1/24 in) thick sheet and cut out a 25mm (1 in) circle using the cutter or template. Stand a marble on a piece of scrap clay to steady it and press the circle onto the marble to make a bowl. Pull one side away from the marble into a lip as a pouring spout. Leave on the marble to bake.

Step 9

Cut two thin strips of clay from a 1.5mm (1/16 in) thick sheet, about 2mm (1/12 in) wide and 25mm (1 in) long. Apply in a cross to the second marble as shown and set aside, steadied with a piece of scrap clay, to bake.

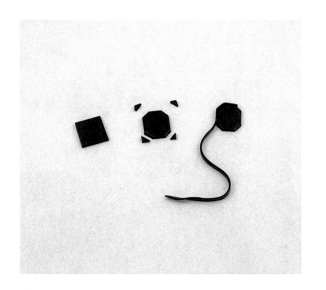

Step 10

Make the weight platform by cutting a 10mm (3/8 in) square from 1mm (1/24 in) thick clay sheet, trimming the corners as shown and applying a strip of clay round the edges to neaten.

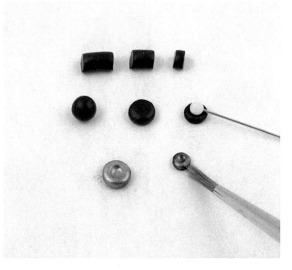

Step 11

Make the weights by forming balls of several sizes and pressing them lightly to flatten. Indent the centres with a ball headed pin. Brush with gold powder before baking or with gold acrylic paint after baking.

Bake all the pieces for 20 minutes.

Step 12

Paint the bowl with gold paint and paint decorative gold details onto the base of the scales and the cross piece. Remove the pin from the balance bar ready for assembly. Varnish all the pieces.

Step 13

Assemble the balance bar by pushing the pin
through the first upright of the cross piece,
through the hinge and then through the
second upright. The hinge should be on the
bottom of the balance bar. Nip off the
protruding part of the pin with cutting pliers.

Step 14

Glue the weight platform and the bowl holder
to each end of the cross piece. Glue the cross
piece to the two platforms. The balance bar
should rock evenly, pivoting on the pin.

Place the bowl in the bowl holder.

Step 15

The finished scales look wonderful
in a dolls house kitchen. Display
them with kitchen ingredients in
the bowl and the weights on the
weight platform. Try embedding
small pieces of metal such as tiny
ball bearings in the weights to
make them heavier - this will
make the scales balance more
realistically.

WIND UP GRAMOPHONE

I love making miniatures that actually work in some way and while this little gramophone does not actually play, it has a handle that winds and records that can be put on and off. It also has an arm with a tiny needle that you can lift on and off the record. Gramophones of this kind (normally called phonographs in the USA) were popular in the early part of the 20th century and the advert for His Master's Voice gramophones with the image of a little dog listening into the horn is an icon of the 1920's and 1930's.

Expertise level: Advanced

Height of model: approximately 6cms (2 5/8 in)

TOOLS AND MATERIALS

- Polymer Clay - dark brown, black - about 1/2 a 56g (2oz) block of each. Small quantities of leaf green
- Copper coloured wire, 0.8mm (20 ga.) thick approx. - about 15cms (6 in)
- Pencil
- Circle cutters - 30mm (1 1/4 in), 25mm (1 in) and 20mm (3/4 in) - or draw circles of these diameters on card and cut out to use as templates
- Paperclip
- PVA glue

- Sandpaper
- 1mm drill bit
- A brass lace-making pin or ordinary dressmakers' pin (brass pins are easier to cut)
- Superglue
- Wire cutters or cutting pliers
- Copper powder or acrylic paint
- Soft paintbrush
- Acrylic varnish or polymer clay varnish
- Gramophone templates traced and cut out. Record labels printed and cut out.

TEMPLATES AND RECORD LABELS FOR THE GRAMOPHONE

Photocopy the images and print out at exactly the size indicated. Alternatively you can download the images from www.sueheaser.com and print them out from your computer (see instructions on page 5.)

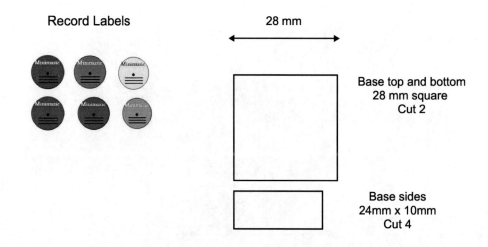

Record Labels

28 mm

Base top and bottom
28 mm square
Cut 2

Base sides
24mm x 10mm
Cut 4

Step 1

THE HORN

Form a 20mm (3/4 in) ball of black clay and shape into a teardrop. Flatten the wide end and push the point of a pencil into it. Use the pencil to shape the clay into a funnel shape. Now pinch all round the edges of the funnel with your thumb and forefinger to thin the clay and widen the funnel into a horn. Press the pencil against the clay all round the inside of the horn to make shallow grooves and shape it.

Step 2

Press the horn, face down onto a work surface and press all round the edges to thin it further. Use a 30mm (1 1/4 in) cutter to cut out the horn neatly. If you use a template instead, cut out the circle in a piece of card and slip the piece of card over the top of the horn to cut round the inside of the circle. Decorate the horn by pressing the end of a paperclip onto both the inside and the outside of the rim.

Step 3

Trim the point of the horn and pierce deeply with a darning needle to make a hole for the wire support. Brush over the clay with copper powder (or you can paint with copper acrylic paint after baking). Bake the horn, with its opening down, on a piece of paper or baking parchment laid on a baking sheet or tile to prevent shiny marks. Varnish the powder when cool.

Step 4

THE GRAMOPHONE BASE

Roll out dark brown clay into a sheet, 2mm (1/12 in) thick (or use the wood grain mixture from the Grandfather Clock project). Lay the sheet on a tile and place the templates on it. Use a slicer blade to cut out the pieces for the gramophone base, leaving them on the tile to bake. Run your finger along the edges of the base top and bottom to chamfer them a little. Bake all the pieces on the tile and remove when cool.

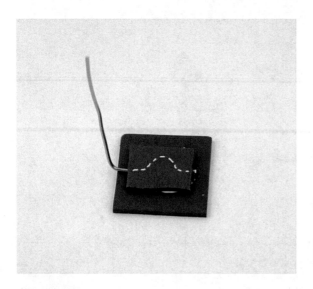

Step 5

Cut a rectangle from a fresh sheet of dark brown clay, 18mm x 15mm (3/4 in x 1/2 in) and 2mm (1/12 in) thick. Cut a piece of wire 9cms (3 1/2 in) long and bend the first 3cms (1 1/4 in) at a right angle. Bend a kink in the 3cm section as shown by the dotted line so that it will lay flat and not twist when secured under the rectangle.

Apply PVA glue to the top of the baked base bottom and place the bent end of the wire flat on the centre of the base with the remainder sticking up vertically. Press the rectangle of fresh clay on top, trapping the wire. Press down firmly all round the wire, the glue will act as a key to the fresh clay to make a strong bond when baked. Trim away any excess clay so that there is a border of at least 3mm (1/8 in) all round. Bake again. This will hold the supporting wire for the horn upright.

Step 6

Trim the inside upright edges of the four side panels at an angle to chamfer them so that they will meet in a right angle when assembled.

Step 7

Rub the chamfered edges on sandpaper to straighten them if necessary and use superglue to glue the four panels together into a box.

Step 8

Make a hole in the centre of one panel by twisting the drill bit with your hand (it will drill easily - no need for a drill). Cut out a notch as shown in the other side - this will fit over the wire support.

Step 9

THE TONE ARM

This is the arm that holds the needle and transmits the sound from the record to the horn. Form a 3mm (1/8 in) ball of black clay and press it onto the tile to make a disk about 6mm (1/4 in) across. Decorate all round with the eye of a needle. Make a similar disk and press the cut-off point of a brass pin onto it so that the point protrudes. Press the first disk on top, trapping the pin point to represent the needle of the gramophone.

Step 10

Form a log, 3mm (1/8 in) thick and 20mm (3/4 in) long. Push into an 'S' shape as shown. Cut another length of the same log, about 3mm (1/8 in) long and pierce through it with a large darning needle. Press the disks with the needle onto one end and the pierced log vertically onto the other. The needle should point straight down. Make sure that the hole in the log is open. Leave black or brush with copper powder if you prefer.

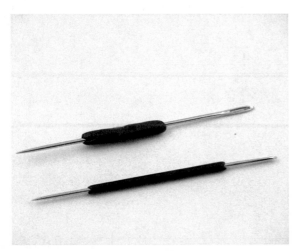

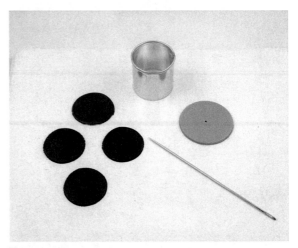

Step 11

THE HANDLE COVER

Pierce a small log of black clay with a darning needle and roll back and forth on your work surface to make a log with the needle inside. It should be at least 25mm (1 in) long and about 2mm (1/12 in) thick. You may need to squeeze it back onto the needle at first if it pulls away as you roll. After baking, this will be cut up and used to cover the wire handle and as a support for the arm.

Step 12

RECORDS AND TURNTABLE

Roll out black clay very thinly (about 1mm (1/24 in) or less), and lay on a tile. Cut out several circles with the 20mm (3/4 in) cutter for records. Leave on the tile for baking.

Roll out a 1.5mm (1/16 in) thick sheet of leaf green for the turntable and cut out a circle with a 25mm (1 in) cutter. Pierce the centre of all the circles with a needle, as centrally as possible. After baking any rough edges on the records can be smoothed with fine sandpaper. Bake on the tile, with the needle arm and the handle.

Step 13

HANDLE ASSEMBLY

Bend a 13mm (1/2 in) piece of wire into a double bend as shown. Remove the black handle from the darning needle. You may need to hold the needle with pliers and twist firmly to remove the clay tube. Cut two lengths from the tube and push one over the end of the wire for the handle. Push the other end of the wire through the hole in the front of the gramophone base and push on the other piece of tube to secure the handle to the base. It should now wind freely.

Step 14

THE BASE ASSEMBLY

Glue the base side panels onto the base bottom, aligning the groove with the wire. Glue the green turntable to the base top and glue the top to the top of the side panels. Glue a small length of brass pin into the hole in the middle of the turntable as a spindle.

Step 16

THE RECORDS

Cut out the record labels carefully. Push a needle through the hole in each record and thread on the paper label, making sure that you pierce it right in the middle. Glue the paper in place and remove the needle.

Finally, put on a record and listen hard!

Step 15

Push another small length of black tube onto the wire and push down until it is just above the top of the base. It should be tight enough to hold, but if it is too loose, glue with superglue. Thread the arm onto the wire with the needle facing down and then trim the wire so that the horn can be pushed on to the wire to rest a little above the arm. Glue the horn in place.

The completed wind-up gramophone. The records can be taken on and off and the tone arm lifted onto the record. The handle can be wound.

MATERIALS AND TECHNIQUES

POLYMER CLAY

Polymer Clay is a highly versatile modelling
material that is hardened by baking in the
home oven. Once baked it is permanent and
can be cut, glued, painted or added to and re-
baked. It comes under the brand names of
Fimo, Premo Sculpey, Cernit, Kato Clay and
Cernit to name some of those most widely
available. Polymer Clay is sold in a wide
range of colours and these can be mixed
together to make further colours. They can
also be partially mixed to give streaked or
marbled effects.

You can use any brand of polymer clay for the
projects in this book. Strong, firm clays such as Premo Sculpey and Fimo Classic or Fimo
Professional work best.

WORKING WITH POLYMER CLAY

Conditioning the clay: Always work each piece of polymer clay in your hands before use to soften
it. Cut a piece off the block and roll it into a log, fold the log in half and roll again. Repeat until
the clay folds easily without cracking.

Pieces can be pressed together lightly to effect a join and will fuse together during baking. Keep
your work surface clean by wiping with wet wipes.

MEASURING

Use a ruler to measure the clay pieces constantly
while you work to ensure that you are keeping
each model to scale. To measure logs and balls,
you can cut out square notches in the side of a
piece of card of the different widths that you need
a lot. Then you can roll a ball or log and hold the
correct notch over the clay to check it is the right
size. Measurements are given in metric and
imperial equivalents. Sometimes these are not
precise conversions to the inches when an
approximation is all that is needed.

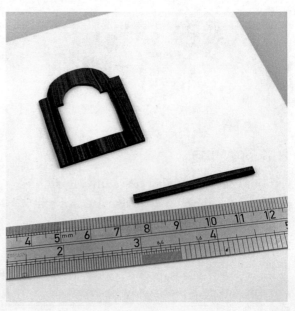

74

BAKING

Bake all pieces in an ordinary domestic oven according to the manufacturers' instructions. This is normally between 110°C and 130°C (230°F and 270°F). I usually bake all miniatures for 20 - 30 minutes. Pieces that are built and baked on a tile should be put in the oven on their tile without attempting to move them to avoid distorting the pieces. Bake other pieces on a baking tray that has been lined with a sheet of baking parchment or plain paper to avoid any shiny patches where they touch the baking sheet. The clay will not become fully hardened until it has cooled down after baking.

GLUING POLYMER CLAY

Use Superglue to glue together pieces of baked polymer clay. The glue makes a very strong bond. The type that gives you 5 - 10 seconds of setting time is preferable so you can reposition if necessary before it sets. White PVA glue or Tacky glue is best for gluing paper or fabric to baked polymer clay.

VARNISHING AND PAINTING

For pieces that require varnishing, use a polymer clay varnish, or an acrylic water-based varnish. Other varnishes may not set properly on polymer clay. Water based acrylic paints are the kind to use for painting details on polymer clay. It is best to de-grease the surface before painting by brushing with methylated spirits (rubbing alcohol) or the paint may not stick well.

SAFETY

Polymer clay is very safe to use and has a non-toxic label worldwide. It is safe to bake in your home oven and for children to use. Avoid burning the clay which will happen if your oven rises over about 170°C (340°F). Like any burning plastic, the smoke smells unpleasant and should not be inhaled. If this happens, turn off the oven and ventilate the room well.

TOOLS AND EQUIPMENT

Most equipment will be at hand in your own home. The following items are the basic tools you will need when making polymer clay miniatures.

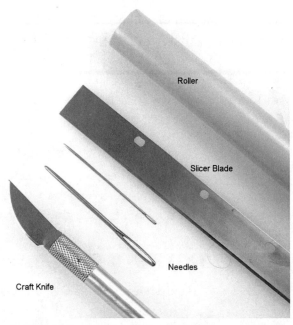

Work surface: A smooth melamine chopping board is ideal, or else a ceramic tile or a cutting mat.

Craft knife: A curved blade like the one shown above is the most versatile.

Ruler: To measure the pieces of clay as you work so that the models are to scale.

Slicer blades: (Long straight blades) Invaluable for cutting straight edges on sheets of clay.

Rolling tools: A small acrylic or nylon rolling pin is the best type or you can improvise with a small bottle or jam jar. For even rolling, place two strips of thick card of the required thickness on either side of the clay as you roll it out. A pasta machine is not essential but is great fun and speeds up rolling and conditioning.

Large needles: Use blunt-pointed tapestry or wool needles for sculpting and indenting lines. A darning needle or pin is used to make holes.

Baking tray: Covered with non-stick baking parchment or ordinary paper for baking the clay.

Ceramic tile: Use for making pieces that can be created and baked on the tile without moving them so as to avoid distortion. Tiles are available from DIY stores.

Wet Wipes: For cleaning hands and work surfaces.

Oven: Your home oven is fine for baking polymer clay. A fan oven is ideal or any electric oven. Gas ovens and ranges such as Agas should be used with an oven thermometer to check the temperature.

Cutters: Many projects use several sizes of circle cutters from 6mm (1/4 in) to 40mm (1 1/2 in). Cutter sets are always useful for making polymer clay miniatures and are available from cake decorating and kitchen stores as well as many polymer clay suppliers. Alternatively you can improvise by drawing a circle on card with a pair of compasses to the correct diameter and cutting out the circle. Lay this template on the sheet of clay and cut round with a knife. Another option is to use a plastic circle templates sheet available from graphics and drawing equipment suppliers.

POLYMER CLAY SUPPLIERS

Polymer clay is available in art and craft shops throughout the world. There are also many mail order suppliers on the web. Search on "polymer clay" or on the brand of your choice. The following are recommended mail order suppliers and they all have tools and accessories as well.

UK SUPPLIERS
www.clayaround.co.uk
www.polymerclay.co.uk

US SUPPLIERS
www.polymerclayexpress.com
www.clayfactory.net

AUSTRALIAN SUPPLIERS
www.polymerclay.com.au

NEW ZEALAND SUPPLIERS
www.zigzag.co.nz

OTHER SUPPLIERS

www.finecutsugarcraft.com - UK site for tiny cutters
www.clayfactory.net - US site for tiny cutters
www.lazertran.com - for Lazertran papers world wide
Doll Artist's Workshop: www.minidolls.com - miniature haberdashery USA
www.britishminiatures.co.uk - lists of dolls house materials suppliers UK

USEFUL WEBSITES

British Polymer Clay Guild: www.bpcg.org.uk

International Polymer Clay Guild (USA): www.theipca.org

Polymer Clay Central: www.polymerclaycentral.com
(Many tutorials, swaps, ideas, huge archive)

Sculpey website: www.sculpey.com
(Lots of free projects)

Facebook: search on miniatures and polymer clay: www.facebook.com

Sue Heaser is a specialist in polymer clays and metal clays and has written 15 internationally published books on these and other craft subjects. She teaches workshops all over the world. For information on Sue, her books and her work as well as free projects, tips and resources, see her website:

www.sueheaser.com

INDEX

Made in the USA
San Bernardino, CA
16 March 2016